Table of Contents

Introduction

Welcome to "The Ultimate Guide on How to Start a Party Planning Business." In this comprehensive guide, we're going to dive deep into the vibrant and exhilarating world of party planning. We'll provide you with all the tools, knowledge, and insider tips you need to launch a successful party planning business. So, let's get started on this exciting journey together!

Chapter 1: Introduction to Party Planning

Party planning is not just about organizing events; it's about crafting unforgettable experiences, spreading joy, and creating memories that last a lifetime. As a party planner, you have the unique ability to bring visions to life and make ordinary moments extraordinary. With the growing demand for professional party planning services, there's never been a better time to enter this flourishing industry. People are increasingly seeking expert help to ensure their events are flawlessly executed, allowing them to enjoy their celebrations without the stress of planning and coordination.

Chapter 2: Assessing Your Skills and Qualifications

Before you jump into the world of party planning, it's essential to take a step back and assess your skills and qualifications. Think about your background, education, and experience in event planning, hospitality, or related fields. Identify your strengths within party planning – do you excel in themed parties, weddings, or corporate events? By evaluating your expertise, you can pinpoint the types of parties and events you're best suited to plan and deliver exceptional results.

Chapter 3: Understanding Your Target Market

A key component of building a successful party planning business is understanding your target market. Who are your ideal clients? Are they individuals, families, or businesses? Conduct thorough market research to uncover the needs, preferences, and budget considerations of your potential clients. This knowledge will enable you to tailor your services to meet their specific requirements and exceed their expectations.

Chapter 4: Developing Your Business Plan

Every successful business begins with a well-thought-out business plan. In this chapter, we'll guide you through the process of creating a solid foundation for your party planning venture. Outline your business goals, mission statement, and core values. Define the services you'll offer, your pricing structure, and revenue projections. Additionally, we'll explore how to develop an effective marketing strategy to reach and attract your target audience. A robust business plan will serve as your roadmap to success, keeping you focused and organized as you grow your business.

Chapter 5: Legal and Regulatory Considerations

Navigating the legal and regulatory landscape is crucial for any business owner. As a party planner, you'll need to understand the permits, licenses, and contracts necessary for operating your business. This chapter will provide a comprehensive overview of the legal requirements, including compliance with event planning regulations, liability considerations, and insurance needs. We'll also discuss the importance of obtaining liability insurance to protect your business and your clients.

Chapter 6: Setting Up Your Business Operations

Smooth operations are the backbone of any successful business. In this chapter, we'll guide you through the essential steps to set up your party planning business. We'll discuss choosing a business structure, registering your business, and setting up your office space. Additionally, we'll cover establishing a technology infrastructure, developing administrative systems, and creating policies and procedures for client contracts, payments, and vendor relationships. By setting up efficient operations, you'll be well-prepared to deliver exceptional service and manage your business effectively.

Stay tuned for the upcoming chapters as we continue to explore the exciting world of party planning. Whether you're an aspiring entrepreneur or looking to expand your existing event planning business, this guide will provide you with valuable insights and strategies for success. Get ready to embark on a journey filled with creativity, joy, and celebration.

Chapter 1: Introduction to Party Planning

Hey there! Welcome to the world of party planning! If you've ever wondered how to turn your passion for organizing and celebrating into a career, you're in the right place. Party planning isn't just about throwing a good bash; it's about creating unforgettable moments that people will cherish forever. Whether it's a birthday party, a wedding, a corporate event, or any special occasion, professional party planners are the magicians behind the scenes making sure everything is perfect.

Defining Party Planning

So, what exactly is party planning? Imagine being the mastermind who takes an idea and turns it into a spectacular event. Party planning involves orchestrating every little detail, from the initial concept and design to the actual execution and even the follow-up. It's about choosing the right venue, crafting a theme that fits the occasion, managing invitations, coordinating with vendors, and ensuring the event flows seamlessly.

A successful party planner is like a meticulous artist, paying attention to every brushstroke to ensure the final masterpiece is flawless. Every element, no matter how small, contributes to the overall success of the event, providing an unforgettable experience for everyone involved.

The Increasing Demand for Professional Party Planning Services

You might be wondering why there's such a buzz around professional party planning services these days. Well, several factors have led to this increasing demand:

Busy Lifestyles: In our fast-paced world, people are busier than ever. Juggling work, family, and social commitments leaves little time to plan and execute a flawless event. That's where professional party planners come in, taking the stress off their clients' shoulders so they can simply enjoy the celebration.

Desire for Personalization: Today, everyone wants their event to stand out. Whether it's a corporate brand looking to impress or a couple planning their dream wedding, there's a growing demand for unique, personalized experiences. Party planners bring creativity and innovation to the table, helping clients craft one-of-a-kind themes and unforgettable moments.

Expertise and Knowledge: Party planners are pros who know the ins and outs of the industry. They stay up-to-date with the latest trends, technologies, and best practices. This expertise ensures that every event they handle is well-organized and delivers outstanding results.

Attention to Detail: A great party planner leaves nothing to chance. They're all about the details, meticulously handling logistics, coordinating with vendors, and managing the event flow. This attention to detail ensures that everything runs smoothly, providing a seamless and enjoyable experience for everyone.

The Purpose and Structure of This Guide

So, what can you expect from this guide? Our goal is to equip aspiring party planners like you with all the knowledge and tools you need to start and run a successful party planning business. Each chapter will delve into a specific aspect of the party planning process, offering valuable insights, practical tips, and proven strategies to help you navigate the industry.

By the end of this guide, you'll have a solid understanding of the party planning landscape, the skills required to thrive, and the steps to take to establish and grow your own business.

We're excited to embark on this journey with you!

Now, let's move on to Chapter 2, where we'll explore how to assess your skills and qualifications in party planning. Ready? Let's dive in!

Chapter 2: Assessing Your Skills and Qualifications

So, you're excited about starting your own party planning business! That's fantastic! But before you dive headfirst into this thrilling venture, it's essential to take a step back and assess your skills and qualifications. This chapter is all about understanding your background, education, and experience to pinpoint your strengths and areas of expertise within party planning. By doing this, you'll be better equipped to identify the types of parties and events you're most qualified to plan. Let's walk through this process together, shall we?

Evaluate Your Background, Education, and Experience

First things first, let's take a look at your background, education, and experience. This is a crucial step in determining how well-suited you are for a party planning business. Reflect on your previous work experiences, educational achievements, and any relevant training or certifications you've acquired.

Think about how these experiences have prepared you with the skills and knowledge necessary for party planning. If you have a background in event planning, hospitality, or a related field, you might already have a solid foundation to build upon. Consider any previous roles where you were involved in organizing events, managing logistics, or coordinating with vendors and suppliers. These experiences can significantly boost your credibility as a party planner.

Identify Your Strengths and Areas of Expertise

Every party planner has unique strengths and areas of expertise within the industry. Recognizing these strengths is vital because they will help differentiate your business and attract clients who appreciate your specific skills.

Take some time to consider the aspects of party planning where you excel. Are you a whiz at designing and creating themed parties? Do you have a talent for organizing weddings and coordinating with various vendors like florists, caterers, and photographers? Or maybe you're experienced in planning corporate events and handling the particular demands and needs of businesses?

By understanding your strengths and areas of expertise, you can position yourself as a specialist in those particular types of parties or events. This specialization will not only set you apart from the competition but also help you attract clients who are specifically looking for the skills you offer.

Determine the Types of Parties and Events You Are Qualified to Plan

Now that you have a good grasp of your strengths, it's time to be realistic about the types of parties and events you're qualified to plan. Consider your skill set, expertise, and resources when determining which types of events you feel confident in organizing and delivering exceptional results for.

For instance, themed parties, like children's birthday parties or holiday gatherings, require a lot of creativity and attention to detail. If you love crafting unique themes and creating memorable experiences, these types of parties might be right up your alley.

Weddings, on the other hand, are complex events that demand extensive planning and coordination. If you have experience in wedding planning or a deep understanding of the wedding industry, specializing in weddings could be a lucrative niche for you.

Corporate events, such as conferences, product launches, and business meetings, have their own unique set of requirements. If you have experience in the corporate world or expertise in managing large-scale events, focusing on corporate event planning might be the perfect path for you.

By determining the types of parties and events you are qualified to plan, you can concentrate your efforts on honing your skills and marketing your services to the right target audience.

Looking Ahead

In the next chapter, we'll delve into understanding your target market and conducting market research to effectively attract clients who are seeking the specific services you offer. So, stay tuned and get ready to take your party planning business to the next level!

Chapter 3: Understanding Your Target Market

Hey there, party planners! Let's dive into one of the most critical aspects of building a successful party planning business: understanding your target market. Knowing who your ideal clients are and what they want is key to tailoring your services and standing out in a competitive industry. In this chapter, we'll explore how to define your target market segments, conduct effective market research, and identify opportunities to differentiate your business.

Defining Your Target Market Segments

First things first, let's talk about defining your target market segments. This step is all about figuring out which specific groups within the party planning industry you want to serve. Your target segments could include individuals, families, or businesses, each with their unique needs, preferences, and budget considerations.

When defining your target segments, consider factors such as age, gender, income level, and location. For instance, if you're passionate about planning children's birthday parties, your target market segment would be parents of young children. On the flip side, if you're more interested in organizing corporate events, your focus would shift to businesses and organizations.

Think about the specifics: Are you targeting young professionals planning milestone birthday parties? Or maybe families looking for someone to handle their annual holiday gatherings? The clearer you are about who you want to serve, the better you can tailor your services to meet their needs.

Conducting Market Research

Once you've nailed down your target market segments, it's time to roll up your sleeves and dive into some market research. This step is crucial for gaining a deep understanding of your audience's needs, preferences, and budget considerations.

Start by conducting surveys, interviews, or focus groups with individuals or organizations that fit your target market. Ask them about their past experiences with party planning services, their expectations for future events, and any challenges they've faced. These insights will be incredibly valuable in shaping your business strategy.

Don't forget to scope out the competition. Take a good look at what other party planners in your area are offering. Analyze their pricing, the services they provide, and who their target market is. This will help you identify gaps in the market and opportunities for differentiation. For example, maybe you notice that no one in your area offers eco-friendly party planning services or themed parties for specific cultural celebrations. These could be unique niches you could fill.

Identifying Opportunities for Differentiation

As you gather information from your market research, you'll start to see opportunities for differentiation within your chosen segments. Standing out from the competition is essential, and there are several ways to do this.

Consider specializing in a specific theme or type of event that's in high demand but not widely offered by other planners. This could be anything from rustic barn weddings to high-tech corporate retreats. By becoming an expert in a niche area, you can attract clients looking for something unique and specialized.

Your level of service can also set you apart. Maybe you offer personalized consultations where you take the time to understand every detail of your client's vision. Or perhaps you excel in creating custom decorations and unique entertainment options that other planners don't offer.

Creativity is another powerful differentiator. If you can bring innovative ideas to the table and execute them flawlessly, you'll build a reputation for delivering memorable and distinctive events.

By thoroughly understanding your target market's needs, preferences, and budget considerations, and identifying opportunities to differentiate your services, you'll be well-positioned to thrive in the party planning industry.

In the next chapter, we'll take all this valuable information and discuss how to develop your business plan to turn your ideas into a profitable venture. Ready to get started? Let's make your party planning dreams a reality!

Chapter 4: Developing Your Business Plan

Creating a well-thought-out business plan is crucial for the success of any party planning business. Think of it as your roadmap, providing clear direction and keeping you focused on your goals. In this chapter, we'll walk through the steps of developing your business plan, from outlining your goals and mission statement to defining your services, pricing structure, revenue projections, and marketing strategy. Ready? Let's dive in!

Outline Your Business Goals

Start by identifying your business goals. What do you hope to achieve with your party planning business? It's important to set both short-term and long-term goals that are specific, measurable, attainable, relevant, and time-bound (SMART). For instance, your short-term goal could be to book your first five clients within the next three months. Meanwhile, a long-term goal might be to establish yourself as the go-to party planner in your area within the next five years. By setting these goals, you'll have clear targets to aim for and a way to measure your progress.

Define Your Mission Statement

Your mission statement defines the purpose and values of your business. It should reflect your passion for creating unforgettable experiences and the unique value you bring to the industry. Take some time to craft a concise and impactful mission statement that captures the essence of your party planning business. For example, you might say, "Our mission is to turn ordinary moments into extraordinary memories by delivering exceptional party planning services with creativity, professionalism, and a personal touch."

Establish Your Core Values

Core values are the guiding principles that shape your business culture and decision-making processes. They serve as a framework for how you interact with clients, vendors, and employees. Think about values like professionalism, creativity, attention to detail, and customer satisfaction. These values will provide a foundation for building your brand and delivering exceptional services. When you know what you stand for, it's easier to make decisions that align with your business philosophy.

Define Your Services

Clearly outlining the services you offer as a party planner is essential. Consider the types of events you are qualified to plan, such as weddings, birthdays, corporate events, or themed parties. Be specific about the services you provide, like event design and decor, vendor coordination, budget management, and on-site event management. This clarity will help potential clients understand exactly what you offer and why they should choose you over the competition.

Pricing Structure and Revenue Projections

Developing a pricing structure that is both competitive and profitable is a delicate balance. Consider factors such as your expenses, market demand, and the value of your services. You need to cover your costs while ensuring your services remain attractive to potential clients. Once you have your pricing structure, create revenue projections based on it and your market research. This will help you set realistic financial goals and monitor your progress over time.

Create a Marketing Strategy

A well-designed marketing strategy is essential for reaching and attracting your target market. Think about your target audience's preferences and interests to determine the best channels to promote your services. This might include online marketing through social media platforms, website optimization, content marketing, and email campaigns. Networking within the event planning industry and forming partnerships with vendors and venues can also expand your reach. Remember, your marketing strategy should be dynamic and adaptable as you learn more about what works best for your business.

Putting It All Together

By outlining your business goals, mission statement, core values, services, pricing structure, revenue projections, and marketing strategy, you'll have a clear roadmap for the success of your party planning business. This detailed plan will guide your decision-making and keep you focused on your ultimate goals.

In the next chapter, we will explore the legal and regulatory considerations you need to be aware of when starting your party planning business. But for now, take a moment to reflect on what you've learned here and start putting your plan together. With a solid business plan in place, you're well on your way to creating a thriving party planning business!

Chapter 5: Legal and Regulatory Considerations

Starting a party planning business is incredibly exciting! The thought of organizing and creating memorable events can be thrilling. However, amidst all this excitement, it's crucial not to overlook the legal and regulatory aspects that come with running your own business. This chapter will guide you through the key legal requirements and regulations you need to be aware of to ensure your business operates smoothly and both you and your clients are protected.

Understanding the Legal Requirements

Before you dive headfirst into launching your party planning business, it's essential to get familiar with the legal requirements specific to your location. This includes obtaining all necessary permits, licenses, and drafting proper contracts. Keep in mind that these requirements can vary greatly depending on where you're located, so thorough research is key.

Permits and Licenses

One of the first steps in setting up your party planning business is securing the required permits and licenses. These could range from general business licenses to occupancy permits if you plan on operating from a physical location. Additionally, there might be specific permits related to event planning services. To get a clear picture of what you need, reach out to your local government authorities or the small business administration in your area. They can provide detailed information on the specific permits and licenses necessary for your business.

Contracts and Agreements

When offering party planning services, having well-drafted contracts and agreements is a must. These documents protect both your business and your clients by clearly outlining the terms and conditions of your services. This includes the scope of work, payment terms, cancellation policies, and liability limitations. It's wise to consult with a legal professional to ensure your contracts are comprehensive and enforceable. A solid contract can help prevent misunderstandings and provide a clear framework for your business relationship with clients.

Compliance with Regulations

Beyond obtaining permits and licenses, it's vital to comply with regulations that govern event planning services. These regulations might cover areas like safety, health, privacy, and advertising. Familiarizing yourself with the specific regulations in your jurisdiction and ensuring your business operations align with these requirements is crucial. Staying compliant not only protects your business but also ensures you provide a safe and professional service to your clients.

Liability and Insurance Requirements

Protecting your business and clients from potential liabilities is another important consideration. Liability insurance is a smart investment as it can protect you against accidents, property damage, or injuries that might occur during the events you organize. This type of insurance provides financial protection and peace of mind for both you and your clients, ensuring that unexpected incidents don't derail your business.

Contract Review

Before you finalize contracts with your clients, it's a good practice to have them reviewed by a legal professional. This step ensures that your contracts are legally binding, fair, and protect the interests of all parties involved. A legal review can help catch any potential issues and ensure that your agreements are solid and enforceable.

Conclusion

Understanding and navigating the legal requirements and regulations is a fundamental part of starting and running a successful party planning business. By obtaining the necessary permits and licenses, complying with applicable regulations, and considering liability insurance, you can protect your business and provide a secure and professional service to your clients.

Now that we've covered the legal aspects, let's move on to Chapter 6, where we will discuss how to set up your business operations effectively. Get ready to take your party planning business to the next level!

Chapter 6: Setting Up Your Business Operations

Alright, now that we've covered the essentials, it's time to roll up our sleeves and get down to the nitty-gritty of setting up your business operations. This is a crucial step in establishing a successful party planning business, and we'll go over everything from choosing your business structure to setting up your office space and technology infrastructure. We'll also discuss how to develop policies and procedures for client contracts, payments, and vendor relationships. Let's dive in!

Choosing a Business Structure

One of the first big decisions you'll make is choosing a business structure. This choice will impact how you run your business, your liability, and your taxes. The most common types of business structures are:

- **Sole Proprietorship:** Simple and straightforward, but you're personally liable for business debts.
- **Partnership:** If you're going into business with someone else, this

structure is easy to establish, but again, personal liability is a factor.

- **Limited Liability Company (LLC):** Offers flexibility and protects your personal assets from business debts.
- **Corporation:** More complex and suitable for larger businesses, with limited liability but more regulations.

Each structure has its own benefits and considerations, so it's essential to research thoroughly and consult with a legal professional to determine the best fit for your business.

Registering Your Business

Once you've decided on a business structure, the next step is to register your business with the appropriate authorities. This typically involves obtaining a business license or permits at the local, state, and federal levels. The requirements can vary greatly depending on your location, so it's important to research the specific regulations and procedures in your area. Proper registration ensures you're operating legally and can avoid any potential fines or shutdowns.

Setting Up Your Office Space

Creating a functional and inviting office space is essential for the day-to-day operations of your party planning business. Think about the size and layout of your office, and make a list of the equipment and supplies you'll need to run your business effectively. This might include:

- Desks and chairs
- Computers and printers
- Filing cabinets
- Office software
- Storage for party supplies and decorations

Your office should be a space where you can focus and be productive, so invest in making it both comfortable and efficient.

Establishing Technology Infrastructure

In today's digital age, having a strong technology infrastructure is non-negotiable. You'll need a reliable internet connection, a professional email address, and various software tools that can streamline your operations. Consider investing in:

- **Project Management Software:** To keep track of tasks, deadlines, and project progress.
- **Customer Relationship Management (CRM) Systems:** To manage client information and interactions.
- **Accounting Software:** To handle invoicing, expenses, and financial tracking.

These tools will not only make your life easier but also ensure you provide a professional service to your clients.

Developing Policies and Procedures

To ensure smooth operations and provide excellent service to your clients, it's important to develop clear policies and procedures. These should cover:

- **Client Contracts:** Create standard templates that outline the scope of work, timelines, and terms.
- **Payment Terms and Methods:** Clearly define when and how clients should make payments.
- **Vendor Relationships:** Establish guidelines for working with vendors and suppliers, including contracts and payment terms.

Clear and transparent policies and procedures help protect your business and ensure consistent and professional interactions with clients and vendors.

Putting It All Together

Setting up your business operations requires careful planning and attention to detail. By choosing the right business structure, registering your business properly, setting up a functional office space, establishing a strong technology infrastructure, and developing clear policies and procedures, you'll be well-positioned for success in the party planning industry.

In the next chapter, we will explore how to build your brand and establish an online presence to attract clients and grow your party planning business. Get ready to take your business to the next level!

Chapter 7: Building Your Brand and Online Presence

Hey there, future party planning mogul! In today's digital age, building a strong brand and establishing a solid online presence is absolutely essential for the success of your party planning business. A well-defined brand identity will not only help you stand out from the competition but also attract your target audience and build trust among potential clients. So, let's dive into the key steps to building your brand and creating an effective online presence.

Develop a Strong Brand Identity

Your brand identity is the image, personality, and values that your business represents. It's all about establishing a brand that reflects your creativity, professionalism, and expertise as a party planner. Here are some important considerations when developing your brand identity:

1. **Determine Your Unique Selling Proposition (USP)**: What sets you apart from other party planning

businesses? Maybe you have a knack for organizing themed parties that no one else can match, or perhaps your attention to detail is unparalleled. Highlight these distinctive qualities, services, or experiences that only you can provide.

2. **Define Your Target Audience**: Who are your ideal clients? Are they young parents looking for someone to organize unforgettable birthday parties, or are they corporate clients in need of elegant and seamless event planning? Understanding your audience allows you to tailor your brand messaging and visuals specifically to them.

3. **Choose a Compelling Brand Name and Logo**: Your brand name should be memorable, relevant, and easy to pronounce. A visually appealing logo that represents your business and resonates with your target audience is equally important. This logo will appear on all your marketing materials, so make sure it's something you love.

4. **Craft a Brand Story**: Share your passion, inspiration, and journey as a party planner. Connect with your audience on an emotional level by explaining why you are passionate about creating unforgettable events. This story helps humanize your brand and make it more relatable.

5. **Consistency is Key**: Ensure that your brand messaging, visuals, and tone of voice remain consistent across all marketing channels, including your website, social media, and promotional materials. Consistency builds trust and recognition.

Create a Professional Website

A professional website is the foundation of your online presence. It serves as an online portfolio that showcases your services, past work, and client testimonials. Here are key elements to consider when creating your website:

1. **Design and Layout:** Choose a clean, visually appealing design that reflects your brand identity. Use high-quality images, videos, and graphics to showcase your previous work and highlight the different types of events you specialize in. A well-designed website leaves a lasting impression.
2. **Clear Description of Your Services:** Make it easy for visitors to understand what you offer. Clearly outline the types of parties and events you plan, such as themed parties, weddings, corporate events, or any other niche markets you cater to.
3. **Testimonials and Reviews:** Feature positive testimonials and reviews from

past clients to establish credibility and build trust. Happy clients are your best advocates.

4. **Contact Information and Inquiry Form:** Make it easy for potential clients to reach out to you by providing clear contact information and an inquiry form. Promptly respond to inquiries to demonstrate your professionalism and dedication to customer service.

5. **Mobile Optimization:** Ensure that your website is optimized for mobile devices. More and more people are browsing the internet on their smartphones and tablets, so a mobile-friendly site is essential.

Utilize Social Media and Online Marketing Strategies

In addition to having a professional website, utilizing social media and online marketing strategies is crucial for raising awareness and attracting clients to your party planning business. Here are some effective strategies to consider:

1. **Social Media Presence**: Create profiles on popular social media platforms such as Facebook, Instagram, and Pinterest. Regularly post engaging content that showcases your work,

provides party planning inspiration, and interacts with your audience. Social media is a powerful tool for building your brand and connecting with potential clients.

2. **Content Marketing**: Create valuable, informative, and visually appealing content related to party planning. This could include blog posts, how-to guides, party trends, and DIY tips. Share this content on your website and social media channels to establish yourself as an expert in the field.

3. **Paid Online Advertising**: Consider investing in online advertising campaigns to reach a wider audience. Platforms such as Facebook Ads and Google AdWords allow you to target specific demographics and interests, ensuring that your ads are shown to potential clients who may be interested in your services.

4. **Collaborate with Influencers and Industry Professionals**: Partner with influencers or other professionals in the event planning industry who have a strong online presence. Collaborate on projects, feature each other on social media, and cross-promote each other's businesses to expand your reach.

5. **Engage with Your Audience**: Actively respond to comments, messages, and inquiries on your social

media channels and website. Engaging with your audience builds trust and establishes you as a responsive and attentive party planner.

Building your brand and establishing an online presence takes time and effort, but it's a worthwhile investment for the success of your party planning business. By developing a strong brand identity, creating a professional website, and utilizing social media and online marketing strategies, you will raise awareness, attract clients, and position yourself as a trusted and expert party planner in the industry.

Next, in Chapter 8, we will explore strategies for acquiring clients and networking to grow your party planning business. Get ready to take your business to the next level!

Chapter 8: Acquiring Clients and Networking

Hey there! Welcome to Chapter 8, where we'll dive into the exciting world of acquiring clients and expanding your network as a party planner. Getting new clients and keeping them coming back is essential for your business's growth and success. Plus, effective networking can open doors to valuable partnerships and referrals. So, let's get into some strategies that will help you attract new clients and encourage repeat business.

Develop a Marketing Plan

First things first, you need a solid marketing plan. This will be your roadmap for reaching potential clients and raising awareness about your fantastic party planning services. Let's break it down:

Identify Your Target Market

Who are your ideal clients? Think about their age, gender, income level, location, and event preferences. Understanding these details will help you tailor your marketing messages to resonate with them. For example, if you're targeting young professionals, your messaging will differ from what you'd use to attract parents planning kids' birthday parties.

Utilize Word-of-Mouth Marketing

Never underestimate the power of word-of-mouth marketing. It's one of the most effective and cost-efficient ways to get new clients. Encourage your satisfied clients to spread the word about your services to their friends, family, and colleagues. You can sweeten the deal by offering incentives like discounts or referral bonuses to those who bring in new clients.

Harness the Power of Social Media

In today's digital world, having a strong social media presence is a must. Create accounts on platforms like Facebook, Instagram, and Twitter. Regularly post engaging content related to party planning, event inspiration, and your services. Engage with your audience by responding to comments and messages. Don't forget to use targeted social media advertising to reach an even wider audience.

Collaborate with Influencers and Bloggers

Partnering with influencers and bloggers in the event planning industry can significantly boost your visibility. Look for popular influencers or bloggers whose audience matches your target market. Collaborate on sponsored content, giveaways, or event promotions. This can help increase your brand's reach and attract new clients.

Invest in Online Advertising

Consider putting some money into online advertising to broaden your reach. Platforms like Google Ads, Facebook Ads, and Instagram Ads allow you to target specific demographics and locations, ensuring your ads are seen by people who are more likely to be interested in your services.

Networking with Industry Professionals

Building relationships with other professionals in the event industry is crucial. Here's how you can do it effectively:

Attend Industry Events and Conferences

Participate in industry events and conferences where you can meet other professionals in the event planning industry. These events are great for networking, learning from experts, and keeping up with the latest trends and innovations.

Join Professional Associations

Becoming a member of professional associations or organizations related to event planning can be very beneficial. Attend their networking events, workshops, and seminars. These gatherings are perfect opportunities to meet potential clients and build relationships with industry leaders.

Build Genuine Relationships

When you're networking, focus on building genuine relationships instead of just promoting your business. Take the time to get to know other professionals, ask questions, and offer help or referrals when appropriate. A strong network of trusted contacts can lead to referrals and provide support and collaboration opportunities.

Offer Incentives to Attract and Retain Clients

Incentives can be a great way to attract new clients and encourage them to come back. Here are some ideas:

Promotional Discounts

Offer limited-time discounts on your party planning services to attract new clients. This can be a great way to entice individuals who may have been on the fence about hiring a party planner.

Package Deals

Create package deals that bundle various services like venue selection, catering, and decorations at a discounted price. This can appeal to clients looking for a comprehensive and hassle-free party planning experience.

Incentives for Repeat Business

Reward clients who work with you again by offering incentives such as discounted rates, priority booking, or exclusive add-ons. This can help build loyalty and increase the likelihood of repeat business.

By developing a comprehensive marketing plan, networking with industry professionals, and offering attractive incentives, you can successfully acquire clients and grow your party planning business. Don't forget to continuously track and evaluate your marketing efforts and adjust your strategies as needed. Good luck, and happy planning!

Chapter 9: Providing Exceptional Client Service

Running a successful party planning business hinges on exceptional client service. It's all about embracing a client-centric approach, truly understanding and bringing to life their vision, theme, and budget. By offering guidance throughout the planning process, sharing creative ideas, and presenting personalized recommendations, you can ensure a stress-free experience for your clients and a memorable event.

1. Develop a Client-Centric Approach

To truly shine in client service, you need to put your clients' needs and desires at the forefront. This means taking the time to really listen to their party vision, understanding the theme they have in mind, and being mindful of their budget. By focusing on a client-centric approach, you're able to create a customized event that not only meets but exceeds their expectations.

2. Guide Clients Through the Party Planning Process

Not everyone is an expert in event planning, and that's where you come in. As a party planner, your role is to guide your clients through every step of the process. This includes everything from selecting the perfect venue and choosing the right vendors to creating a detailed timeline and managing all the intricate details. Your guidance can alleviate their stress, making the planning journey smooth and enjoyable.

3. Offer Creative Ideas and Personalized Recommendations

Your creativity and expertise are your greatest assets as a party planner. Use them to offer unique and imaginative ideas for your clients' events. Suggest innovative themes, creative decorations, or interactive entertainment options that can make their party stand out. By tailoring your recommendations to their preferences, you can customize the event to perfectly suit their style and vision.

4. Provide Solutions to Challenges

Planning a party can come with its fair share of challenges. Whether it's dealing with budget constraints, finding an alternative venue, or resolving conflicts with vendors, it's your job to find solutions and overcome these hurdles.

Your ability to problem-solve effectively demonstrates your value to clients and ensures a successful event.

5. Establish Open Communication, Trust, and Transparency

Open communication is key to building trust and maintaining a positive relationship with your clients. Encourage them to share their ideas, concerns, and expectations openly. Be transparent about pricing, contracts, and any limitations. Keep them regularly updated on the progress of the planning process, ensuring clear and timely communication throughout.

Conclusion

Exceptional client service is the cornerstone of a successful party planning business. By developing a client-centric approach, guiding clients through the planning process, offering creative ideas and personalized recommendations, and providing solutions to challenges, you can ensure a positive planning experience and deliver a memorable event. Remember, open communication, trust, and transparency are crucial in building strong relationships with your clients. Happy clients are more likely to recommend your services, contributing to the growth and success of your business.

Chapter 10: Growing Your Party Planning Business

Hey there! Let's chat about how to grow your party planning business, ensuring long-term success and profitability. In this chapter, we'll explore some effective strategies to keep your existing clients happy, generate referrals, expand your services, and stay ahead of industry trends.

Implement Strategies to Retain Existing Clients and Generate Referrals

Keeping your current clients happy is key to growing your business. Satisfied clients not only come back for more but also become your best advocates, spreading the word about your fantastic services. Here's how you can retain and delight your clients:

Provide Exceptional Service

Always aim to exceed your clients' expectations at every step of the party planning process. Actively listen to their needs, communicate regularly, and respond promptly to their inquiries. Be organized, attentive to details, and flexible enough to accommodate their requests. Going above and beyond in your service will leave a lasting impression.

Personalize the Experience

Tailor your services to suit each client's unique requirements and preferences. Show genuine interest in their vision, theme, and budget, and offer creative ideas and personalized recommendations. By going the extra mile to create a customized experience, you'll leave a lasting impression that will keep them coming back.

Foster Strong Relationships

Building strong relationships with your clients is essential for client retention. Take the time to genuinely get to know them, both professionally and personally. Remember important details about their past events, their preferences, and milestones in their lives. This personal touch will make them feel valued and foster a sense of loyalty.

Follow Up

After the event, reach out to your clients to thank them for choosing your services and inquire about their satisfaction. Show interest in their overall experience and address any concerns or suggestions they may have. This not only helps to maintain a positive relationship but also provides an opportunity for improvement.

Implement a Referral Program

Encourage satisfied clients to refer your services to others by offering incentives. Consider providing discounts on future services or other rewards for successful referrals. Word-of-mouth referrals are powerful marketing tools and can bring in high-quality leads.

Expand Your Service Offerings or Target Market Segments

Expanding your service offerings or target market segments can open up new opportunities for growth and revenue. Here's how you can do it:

Research Market Demand

Stay informed about current trends, popular themes, and emerging party ideas. Conduct market research, attend industry conferences, and follow relevant publications and websites. Identify gaps in the market and areas where your expertise and passion align.

Offer New Services

Based on market demand, consider expanding your service offerings. For example, you could offer specialized services for specific types of parties, such as children's birthday parties, destination weddings, or corporate team-building events. This allows you to cater to niche markets and attract clients with specific needs.

Target New Market Segments

Assess your skills and qualifications to determine if you can cater to a broader range of clients. If you primarily focus on individual parties, consider expanding to include corporate events or fundraising galas. This diversification allows you to tap into different markets and reach a wider audience.

Collaborate with Other Event Professionals

Partnering with other event professionals, such as caterers, photographers, or entertainment providers, can help expand your service offerings without needing additional resources. Cross-promote each other's services and leverage each other's networks to attract new clients.

Continuously Invest in Professional Development and Stay Informed

To stay competitive and relevant in the party planning industry, it's crucial to continuously invest in your professional development and stay informed about industry trends. Here are some ways to do that:

Attend Conferences and Workshops

Participate in industry conferences, workshops, and seminars to stay up-to-date with the latest trends, techniques, and best practices. Network with other professionals in the field, share insights, and learn from their experiences.

Join Professional Associations

Consider joining professional associations such as the International Live Events Association (ILEA) or the Wedding International Professionals Association (WIPA). These organizations offer resources, industry insights, and networking opportunities.

Follow Industry Experts

Stay connected with influential party planners and industry experts by following them on social media, reading their blogs, and subscribing to their newsletters. This will keep you informed about emerging party themes, creative ideas, and the latest industry news.

Seek Feedback and Act on It

Regularly request feedback from your clients, vendors, and event attendees. Use this feedback to improve your services, identify areas for growth, and stay ahead of the competition. Actively listen to suggestions and implement changes that align with your business goals.

By implementing these strategies, you can effectively grow and expand your party planning business. Whether it's through exceptional service to retain existing clients, expanding your offerings or target market segments, or continuously investing in your professional development, each step will contribute to your business's success.

So, get out there, wow your clients, and watch your party planning business thrive!